Solve all your Maths problems with CGP!

This fantastic CGP book is the best way to help pupils
get to grips with Year 3 Problem Solving.

It's packed with bite-sized tests that get tougher
as pupils build up their skills. By the end of the book they'll have
practised answering the trickiest of problem-solving questions.

We've even included full answers to every question
— plus a handy chart to check progress too!

What CGP is all about

Our sole aim here at CGP is to produce the highest quality books
— carefully written, immaculately presented and
dangerously close to being funny.

Then we work our socks off to get them out to you
— at the cheapest possible prices.

Published by CGP

Editors: Martha Bozic, Liam Dyer, Samuel Mann, Sean McParland and Caley Simpson

With thanks to Tom Miles and Gail Renaud for the proofreading.

With thanks to Jan Greenway for the copyright research.

ISBN: 978 1 78908 640 9

Clipart from Corel®
Printed by Bell & Bain Ltd, Glasgow.

Based on the classic CGP style created by Richard Parsons.

Text, design, layout and original illustrations © Coordination Group Publications Ltd. (CGP) 2020
All rights reserved.

Photocopying this book is not permitted, even if you have a CLA licence.
Extra copies are available from CGP with next day delivery • 0800 1712 712 • www.cgpbooks.co.uk

Contents

Test 1 2

Test 2 4

Test 3 6

Test 4 8

Test 5 10

Test 6 12

Test 7 14

Test 8 16

Test 9 18

Test 10 20

Test 11 22

Test 12 24

Answers 26

Progress Chart 30

How to Use this Book

- This book contains <u>12 tests</u>, all geared towards improving your problem solving skills.

- Each test is out of <u>9 marks</u> and should take about <u>10 minutes</u> to complete.

- Each test starts with some <u>warm-up questions</u>.

- The tests <u>increase in difficulty</u> as you go through the book.

- <u>Answers</u> and a <u>Progress Chart</u> can be found at the <u>back</u> of the book.

Test 1

Warm up

1. Circle the two calculations that have an answer of 20.

    17 + 5   12 + 8   18 – 9   24 – 4

    2 marks

2. Use two of these number cards to make... ⬚8⬚ ⬚5⬚ ⬚9⬚ ⬚2⬚

    a) ... the smallest even two-digit number.

    .... *1 mark*

    b) ... the biggest odd two-digit number.

    .... *1 mark*

3. Yusuf has 26 socks. 14 of them are grey.

    How many of his socks are **not** grey?

    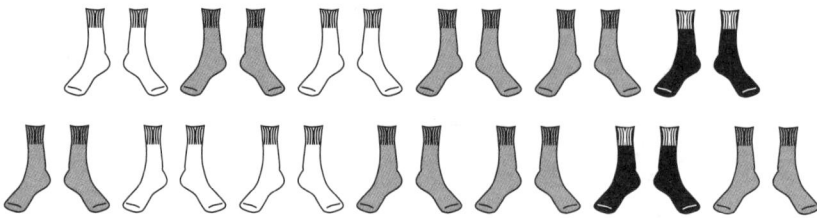

    .... socks *1 mark*

4. Grace doubles a two-digit number.
   Her new number has 2 tens and 4 ones.

   What number did she start with?

   ....
   2 marks

5. The children in a class live in four villages. This table shows how many of the children live in each village.

Village	Children
East Lowing	15
Upper Bury	4
Middling	6
East Highton	7

   How many children live in a village with 'East' in its name?

   .... children
   1 mark

   How many children **do not** live in East Lowing?

   .... children
   1 mark

   END OF TEST

   / 9

Test 2

Warm up

1. What digit is in the tens place in the answer to:

   a) 8 × 5? ....   b) 12 × 5? ....

   2 marks

2. Find the missing number in each calculation.

   20 + **?** = 80   70 − 30 = **?**   **?** + 25 = 45

   ....

   2 marks

3. Zak and Naomi drew these shapes.

   A (rectangle) B (triangle) C (square) D (circle) E (triangle) F (rectangle)

   Zak drew all of the triangles and squares.
   Naomi drew all of the circles and rectangles.

   Write the letter of each shape in the correct box.

   Zak's shapes

   Naomi's shapes

   2 marks

4. Rob sees 43 birds in a tree. 27 of them fly away.

   How many birds are left in the tree?

   .... birds   1 mark

5. *Spuds & Bulbs* sell onions in packs of 2 and potatoes in packs of 5.

   In one day, they sell 8 packs of onions and 10 packs of potatoes.

   How many more potatoes than onions did they sell?

   .... potatoes   2 marks

END OF TEST

/ 9

Test 3

Warm up

1. Draw the next two shapes in this pattern.

   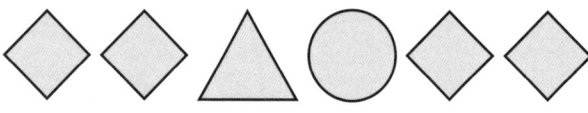 ....

   2 marks

2. Draw lines to join up the calculations that give the same answer.

1 × 5	24 ÷ 2
6 × 2	50 ÷ 5
2 × 5	15 ÷ 3

   2 marks

3. Hafsa says, "8 + 1 = 9, so 80 + 10 = 90."

   For each number in the boxes below, write the number you would add to get an answer of 90.

   Use Hafsa's number fact to help you.

   | 30 | | 20 | | 50 |

   ....

   2 marks

4. Henry has 10 roses. He gives $\frac{1}{5}$ of them away.

How many roses does he give away?

.... roses

1 mark

5. A shop sells these items.

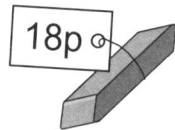 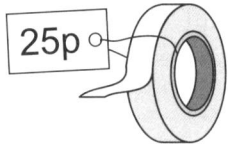

Libby only has 10p coins in her wallet.

How many of her coins will she need to buy one of each item?

.... coins

2 marks

END OF TEST

/ 9

Test 4

Warm up

1. Circle the calculation that gives the biggest answer.

    94 − 80   3 × 4   57 − 47

    _____
    1 mark

2. Cross out the four letters below that have a line of symmetry.

    _____
    2 marks

3. Aaliyah adds two numbers together.

    The first number is 43.

    The second number has 3 fewer ones and 2 fewer tens than the first number.

    What is the sum of the two numbers?

    ....   _____
    2 marks

4. Draw lines to join each shape to the correct description.

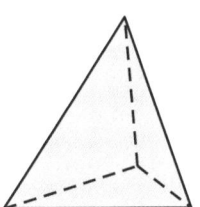 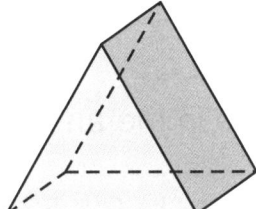 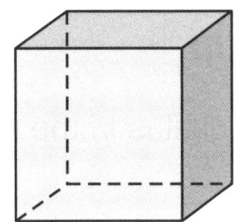

6 faces   6 edges   6 vertices

2 marks

5. The contents of two boxes are shown below.

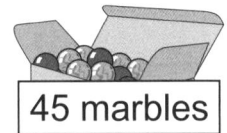 

5 people share the contents of each box equally.

How many more paper clips than marbles does each person get?

.... paper clips

2 marks

END OF TEST

/ 9

Test 5

Warm up

1. What digit is in the ones place in the answer to:

   a) 4 × 4? ....   b) 9 × 5? ....

   2 marks

2. These numbers get bigger by the same amount each time. Fill in the missing numbers below.

   50   150   200   ....

   1 mark

3. A three-digit number is described below.

   The tens digit is half as big as the ones digit. The hundreds digit is odd.

   Which of these numbers could be the number described?

   Tick **all** of the numbers that could be correct.

   ☐ 742   ☐ 348   ☐ 376

   ☐ 612   ☐ 536

   2 marks

4. Circle the shape that has a pair of parallel sides.

1 mark

5. The number of trees in four parks are shown in this table.

Park	Number of trees
A	370
B	435
C	419
D	482

Put the parks in order, starting with the park with the most trees.

....

most ⟶ fewest

1 mark

Ash plants 100 trees in Park D.

How many trees are there in Park D now?

Write your answer in words.

....

2 marks

END OF TEST

/ 9

Test 6

Warm up

1. Use two of these number cards to make... 8 7 5 4 2

   a) ... a multiple of 5, between 40 and 50. .... 1 mark

   b) ... a multiple of 8 that is less than 40. .... 1 mark

2. Tick the correct statements about the shapes below.

   Each shape...

   ... has exactly four sides. ☐

   ... has a pair of parallel sides. ☐

   ... is a pentagon. ☐

   ... has at least two right angles. ☐

   2 marks

3. Draw a shape that has two more sides than a square in the box below.

   1 mark

4. Shade in the same number of circles and squares so that $\frac{1}{3}$ of the shapes are shaded in total.

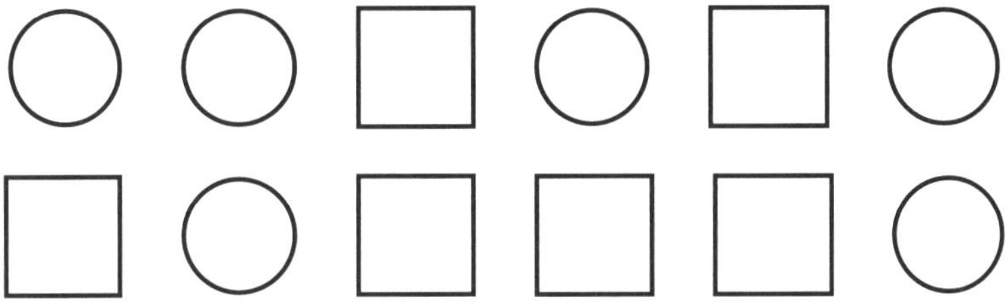

2 marks

5. Katie is at the corner shop.
She only has £1 coins, 10p coins and 1p coins in her purse.

She buys a magazine for £2.35 using exactly 10 coins.

How many of each coin does she use?

.... × £1

.... × 10p

.... × 1p

2 marks

END OF TEST

/ 9

Test 7

Warm up

1. What number is 5 more than the answer to:

    a) 42 + 20? ....   b) 54 − 30? ....

    2 marks

2. Complete each of these calculations with 1-digit numbers.

    a) .... × .... = 27   b) .... ÷ .... = 5

    2 marks

3. Draw lines to join each shape to the number of right angles it has.

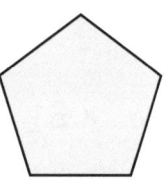

exactly one

exactly four

none

exactly two

2 marks

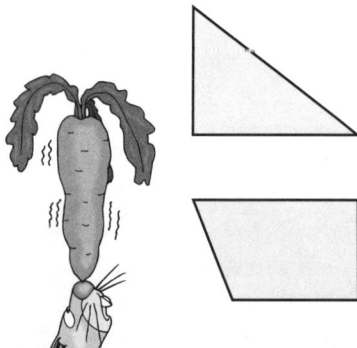

4. Three people share a bowl of ice cream.
Lyra eats one sixth of the ice cream.
Phoebe eats one third. Ibrahim eats one fifth.

Who eats the least amount of ice cream?

....

1 mark

5. Harvey uses counters to represent three-digit numbers.

He represents 423 with these counters:

What number will be represented if he...

...adds another two grey counters?

....

1 mark

...replaces the white counters with the same number of black counters?

....

1 mark

END OF TEST

/ 9

Test 8

Warm up

1. Circle the number in each pair that is closer to a number in the 8 times table.

   a) 22 or 19   b) 44 or 53

   2 marks

2. Write the number that is halfway between:

   a) 33 and 45 ....   b) 78 and 92 ....

   2 marks

3. Look at the weight on the scales below.

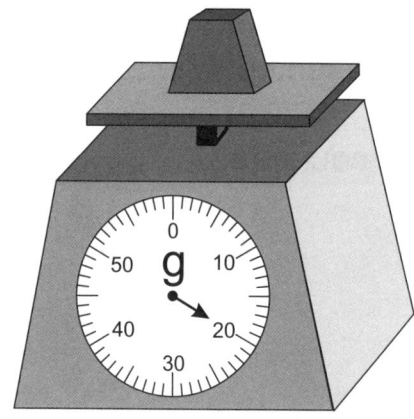

An identical weight is added to the scales.

What mass is shown on the scales now?

.... g

1 mark

4. Look at these numbers cards. 8 4 5 1

Use each card once in the sum below to give the smallest answer possible.

☐☐ + ☐☐ = ...

2 marks

5. A farmer counts all of the animals on her farm and puts her results into a bar chart.

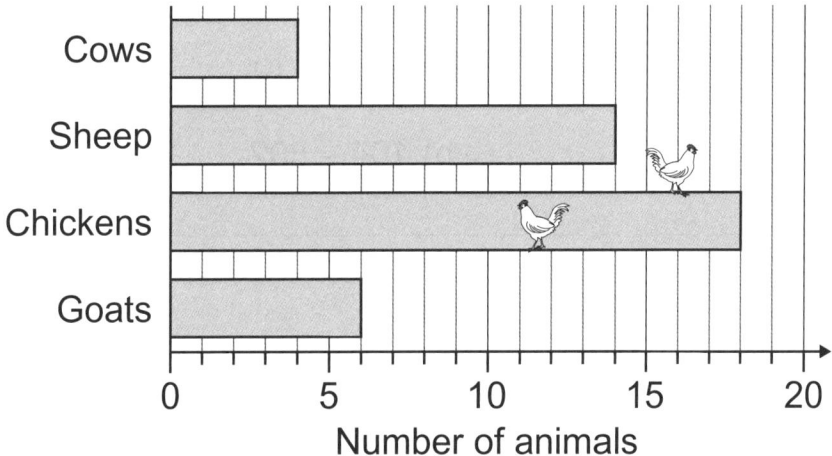

All of her cows and sheep are in a field and all of her chickens and goats are in a barn.

How many more animals are in the barn than in the field?

.... animals

2 marks

END OF TEST

/ 9

Test 9

Warm up

1. Fill in the missing digits to make this sum correct.

    ```
       ☐ 5 3
    +  4 9 6
    ─────────
       6 ☐ 9
       1
    ```

    1 mark

2. What number is equal to half of the answer to:

    a) 128 − 100? ....   b) 104 − 80? ....

    2 marks

3. Carwyn has $\frac{1}{7}$ kg of white rice and $\frac{4}{7}$ kg of brown rice in his cupboard.

    How many kilograms of rice does he have in total?

    .... kg

    1 mark

    He buys another $\frac{2}{7}$ kg of brown rice.

    How many kilograms of brown rice does he have now?

    .... kg

    1 mark

4. In a game, players use the wheel on the right to pick a letter.

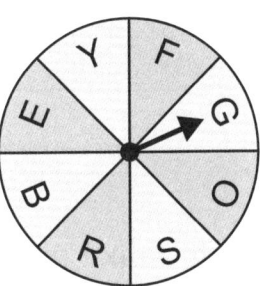

What letter will the arrow be pointing to after a half turn?

....
1 mark

The arrow turns clockwise from Y to O.

Is this turn greater than or less than a right angle?
Circle the correct answer.

greater than a right angle   less than a right angle

1 mark

5. The recipe on the right shows some of the ingredients needed to make one crumble.

Jae-Min is making four crumbles.

How many apples will she need in total?

Jae-Min's Crumble

3 apples

raspberries

.... apples
1 mark

She used 48 raspberries to make four crumbles.

What is the missing number of raspberries in the recipe?

.... raspberries
1 mark

END OF TEST

/ 9

Test 10

Warm up

1. Fill in the gaps to make each calculation correct.

   a) 300 + 30 + 7 = ... + 130 + 7

   b) 600 + ... + 9 = 700 + 20 + 9

   2 marks

2. Circle **all** the odd numbers that are in the 3 times table.

   6   11   15   21   24   29

   1 mark

3. What is the name of the 3D shape shown on the right?

   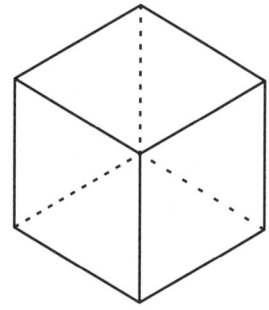

   ....

   1 mark

4. Nev takes 1 minute to complete a puzzle.
   Meg takes 16 fewer seconds to complete the same puzzle.

   How many seconds did Meg take to complete the puzzle?

   .... seconds

   1 mark

5. Four pupils are reading the same book.
The table below shows the fraction
of the book that each pupil has read.

Ada	Ben	Cal	Dev
$\frac{4}{10}$	$\frac{7}{10}$	$\frac{5}{10}$	$\frac{1}{10}$

Put the pupils in order of how much they've read.
Start with the pupil who has read the most.

....

most ⟶ least

1 mark

How much more of the book
has Ben read than Dev?

....

1 mark

6. Emily wants to raise £475 for a local charity.
She raises £124 from her friends
and £289 from her family.

How much more money does she need to raise?

£ ....

2 marks

END OF TEST

/ 9

Test 11

Warm up

1. Fill in the missing numbers on the number line.

   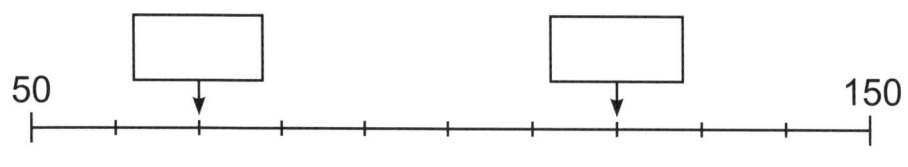

   2 marks

2. Put a tick below the time closest to half past 4.

   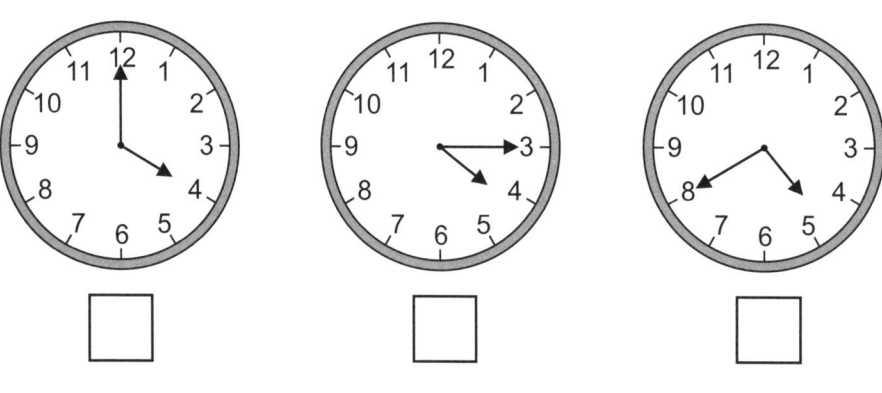

   1 mark

3. Nadia buys these items at a beach shop.

   How much more does she need to spend to reach £20?

   £ ....

   2 marks

4. This pictogram shows the number of pies bought in one day by customers at a pie shop.

Cheese and Onion Pie	⊗ ⊗
Steak Pie	⊗ ◐
Chicken Pie	⊗ ◸
Vegetable Pie	⊗ ⊗ ◐

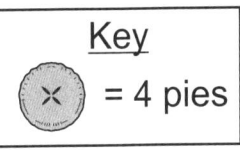
Key
⊗ = 4 pies

How many more vegetable pies were bought than chicken pies?

.... vegetable pies

2 marks

5. Look at this pattern of 30 tiles in Kyle's hallway.

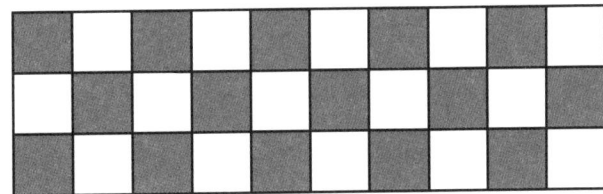

Kyle told the builder he wanted $\frac{6}{10}$ of the tiles to be grey.

How many more of the 30 tiles should have been grey?

.... tiles

2 marks

END OF TEST

/ 9

Test 12

Warm up

1. For each calculation, circle the number in the box that is closest to the correct answer.

   a) 8 × 8 | 54   57   62   65   71 |

   b) 12 × 5 | 48   55   59   62   68 |

   2 marks

2. Fill in the missing digits to complete the calculations.

   a)   1 ☐ 5
         + 3 3 7
         ─────────
            5 0 ☐
            1 1

   b)   9 3 7
         − ☐ 1 1
         ─────────
            4 ☐ 6

   2 marks

3. Ruthie, Gina and Eli share a pack of balloons.

   Ruthie gets $\frac{3}{8}$ of the balloons.

   Gina gets $\frac{2}{8}$ of the balloons.

   What fraction of the balloons does Eli get?

   2 marks

4. A shop sells pens in packs of two and packs of three.
Keiron buys 6 packs of two pens.
Sean buys the same number of pens in packs of three.

How many packs of pens does Sean buy?

.... packs

1 mark

5. A jug of squash is shown on the right.

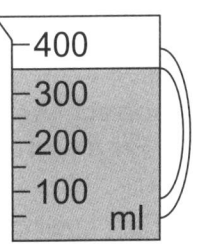

Kim pours out 150 ml of squash for herself.
Jack also pours himself some squash from the same jug.

Afterwards, the jug looks like this.

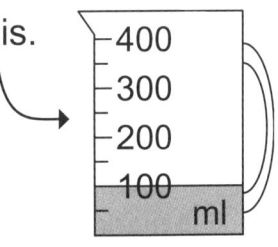

How much squash did Jack pour for himself?

.... ml

2 marks

END OF TEST

/ 9

Answers

Test 1 – pages 2-3

1. 12 + 8 and 24 – 4 should be circled.
   (**2 marks** for both correct calculations circled only, otherwise **1 mark** for one correct and no more than one incorrect calculation circled)
2. a) 28 (**1 mark**)   b) 95 (**1 mark**)
3. 26 – 14 = 12 of his socks are not grey. (**1 mark**)
4. 2 tens + 4 ones = 24,
   so her new number is 24.
   So she started with 24 ÷ 2 = 12.
   (**2 marks** for the correct answer, otherwise **1 mark** for a correct method)
5. 15 children live in East Lowing and 7 children live in East Highton, so 15 + 7 = 22 children live in a village with 'East' in its name. (**1 mark**)

   Add up the children who live in the other three villages.
   4 + 6 + 7 = 10 + 7 = 17 children do not live in East Lowing. (**1 mark**)

Test 2 – pages 4-5

1. a) 4 (**1 mark**)   b) 6 (**1 mark**)
2. 60   40   20
   (**2 marks** for all three correct, otherwise **1 mark** for two correct)
3.
Zak's shapes	Naomi's shapes
B, C, E	A, D, F

   (**2 marks** for all six shapes in the correct boxes, otherwise **1 mark** for at least four shapes in the correct boxes)
4. Partition 27 into 20 and 7 and subtract from 43: 43 – 20 = 23, 23 – 7 = 16
   So there are 16 birds left in the tree. (**1 mark**)
5. They sold 8 × 2 = 16 onions and 10 × 5 = 50 potatoes. Partition 16 into 10 and 6 and subtract from 50:
   50 – 10 = 40, 40 – 6 = 34
   So they sold 34 more potatoes than onions.
   (**2 marks** for the correct answer, otherwise **1 mark** for a correct method)

Test 3 – pages 6-7

1.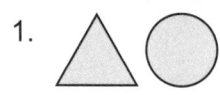

   (**1 mark** for each correct shape)
2. 1 × 5 — 50 ÷ 5
   6 × 2 — 15 ÷ 3
   2 × 5 — 24 ÷ 2
   (**2 marks** for all three lines drawn correctly, otherwise **1 mark** for one correct line)
3. 30 + 60 = 90, 20 + 70 = 90 and 50 + 40 = 90, so the numbers are:
   60   70   40
   (**2 marks** for all three correct, otherwise **1 mark** for two correct)
4. $\frac{1}{5}$ of 10 = 10 ÷ 5 = 2,
   so he gives away 2 roses. (**1 mark**)
5. Add up the prices of the rubber and tape. Partition 25p into 20p and 5p and add to 18p:
   18p + 5p = 23p, 23p + 20p = 43p
   She only has 10p coins, so 4 coins will be 4 × 10 = 40p and 5 coins will be 5 × 10 = 50p. 40p is not enough, so she needs 5 coins.
   (**2 marks** for the correct answer, otherwise **1 mark** for a correct method)

Test 4 – pages 8-9

1. 94 – 80 should be circled. (**1 mark**)
2.

   (**2 marks for all four correct letters only, otherwise 1 mark for at least two correct letters and no more than one incorrect letter**)
3. The first number has 4 tens and 3 ones. So the tens digit of the second number is 4 – 2 = 2 and the ones digit is 3 – 3 = 0. So the second number is 20 and the sum of the two numbers is 43 + 20 = 63.
   (**2 marks for the correct answer, otherwise 1 mark for a correct method**)
4.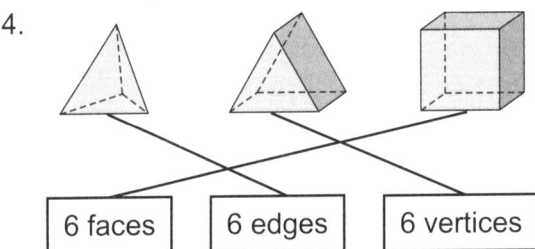

   (**2 marks for all three lines drawn correctly, otherwise 1 mark for one correct line**)
5. Each person gets 45 ÷ 5 = 9 marbles and 60 ÷ 5 = 12 paper clips. So they each get 12 – 9 = 3 more paper clips than marbles.
   (**2 marks for the correct answer, otherwise 1 mark for a correct method**)

Test 5 – pages 10-11

1. a) 6 (**1 mark**)   b) 5 (**1 mark**)
2. 50   100   150   200   250
   (**1 mark for both correct**)
3. Rule out 742 and 376 as the tens digits are not half as big as the ones digits. Rule out 612 as the hundreds digit is even, not odd. This leaves 348 and 536, which should both be ticked.
   (**2 marks for both correct numbers, otherwise 1 mark for one correct number and no more than one incorrect number ticked**)
4.  (**1 mark**)
5. D, B, C, A (**1 mark**)
   482 + 100 = 582, so there are five hundred and eighty-two trees.
   (**2 marks for the correct answer in words, otherwise 1 mark for the correct answer in digits**)

Test 6 – pages 12-13

1. a) 45 (**1 mark**)   b) 24 (**1 mark**)
2. '... has a pair of parallel sides' and '... has at least two right angles' should both be ticked.
   (**2 marks for both correct statements ticked only, otherwise 1 mark for at least one correct statement and no more than one incorrect statement ticked**)
3. E.g.  (**1 mark for any shape with six sides**)
4. There are 12 shapes in total, so $\frac{1}{3}$ of 12 = 12 ÷ 3 = 4 shapes need to be shaded. So 2 circles and 2 squares need to be shaded.
   E.g.
   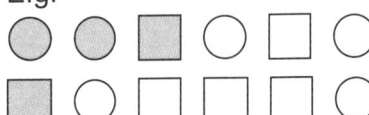

   (**2 marks for any two circles and any two squares shaded, otherwise 1 mark for any four shapes shaded**)

5. £2.35 is £2 and 35p.
So the fewest number of coins she could use is 2 × £1, 3 × 10p and 5 × 1p. This is 2 + 3 + 5 = 10 coins, so must be the correct answer.
(**2 marks for the correct answer, otherwise 1 mark for a correct method**)

Test 7 – pages 14-15

1. a) 67 (**1 mark**) b) 29 (**1 mark**)
2. a) 9 × 3 = 27 or 3 × 9 = 27 (**1 mark**)
   b) 5 ÷ 1 = 5 (**1 mark**)
3.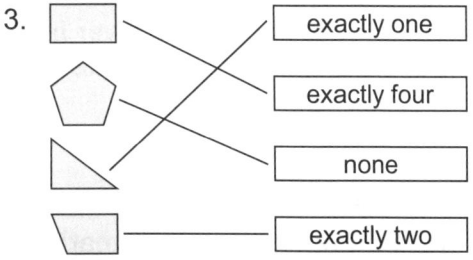

   (**2 marks for all four lines drawn correctly, otherwise 1 mark for two correct lines**)
4. The smallest of the three fractions is one sixth, so Lyra eats the least amount of ice cream. (**1 mark**)
5. The black counters represent hundreds, the grey counters represent tens and the white counters represent ones. There will be 4 hundreds, 4 tens and 3 ones, so the new number will be 443. (**1 mark**)

   There will be 7 hundreds, 2 tens and 0 ones, so the new number will be 720. (**1 mark**)

Test 8 – pages 16-17

1. a) 22 should be circled. (**1 mark**)
   b) 53 should be circled. (**1 mark**)
2. a) 39 (**1 mark**) b) 85 (**1 mark**)
3. The weight has a mass of 20 g. Adding an identical weight brings the mass to 20 + 20 = 40 g. (**1 mark**)
4. To get the smallest answer, the two smallest digits (1 and 4) should be in the tens place and the two biggest digits (5 and 8) should be in the ones place. So the sum could be:
   18 + 45, 45 + 18, 48 + 15 or 15 + 48 (**1 mark**)

   All of these sums add up to 63, so the smallest answer is 63. (**1 mark**)
5. She has 4 cows, 14 sheep, 18 chickens and 6 goats.
   4 + 14 = 18 animals are in the field and 18 + 6 = 24 animals are in the barn.
   So 24 − 18 = 6 more animals are in the barn.
   (**2 marks for the correct answer, otherwise 1 mark for a correct method**)

Test 9 – pages 18-19

1. $\begin{array}{r} 1\ 5\ 3 \\ +\ 4\ 9\ 6 \\ \hline 6\ 4\ 9 \\ {}_1 \end{array}$ (**1 mark**)
2. a) 14 (**1 mark**) b) 12 (**1 mark**)
3. He has $\frac{1}{7} + \frac{4}{7} = \frac{5}{7}$ kg of rice in total. (**1 mark**)

   He has $\frac{4}{7} + \frac{2}{7} = \frac{6}{7}$ kg of brown rice now. (**1 mark**)
4. A half turn is the same as two right angles, so the arrow will be pointing to B. (**1 mark**)

   This turn is greater than a quarter turn, so 'greater than a right angle' should be circled. (**1 mark**)
5. She will need 3 × 4 = 12 apples in total. (**1 mark**)

   She used 48 ÷ 4 = 12 raspberries in each crumble, so 12 is the missing number in the recipe. (**1 mark**)

Test 10 – pages 20-21

1. a) 200 (**1 mark**)   b) 120 (**1 mark**)
2. 15 and 21 should be circled. (**1 mark**)
3. Cube (**1 mark**)
4. 1 minute = 60 seconds, so Meg took 60 − 16 = 44 seconds to complete the puzzle. (**1 mark**)
5. Ben   Cal   Ada   Dev (**1 mark**)
   Ben has read $\frac{7}{10} - \frac{1}{10} = \frac{6}{10}$ more than Dev. (**1 mark**)
6.
   ```
     1 2 4              4 7 5
   + 2 8 9     and    − 4 1 3
   ───────            ───────
     4 1 3                6 2
     ¹ ¹
   ```
   So she needs to raise £62.
   (**2 marks for the correct answer, otherwise 1 mark for a correct method**)

Test 11 – pages 22-23

1. 50   70   120   150
   (**1 mark for each correct answer**)
2. [clock showing time] should be ticked. (**1 mark**)
3. She has already spent £3 + £15 + 99p = £18.99, so she needs to spend another 1p to get to £19 and then another £1 to get to £20. So she needs to spend £1 + 1p = £1.01.
   (**2 marks for the correct answer, otherwise 1 mark for a correct method**)
4. There are two whole symbols and one half symbol for vegetable. One half symbol is 4 ÷ 2 = 2 pies. So 4 + 4 + 2 = 10 vegetable pies are sold in total. There is one whole symbol and one quarter symbol for chicken. One quarter symbol is 4 ÷ 4 = 1 pie. So 4 + 1 = 5 chicken pies are sold in total. So 10 − 5 = 5 more vegetable pies were bought than chicken pies.
   (**2 marks for the correct answer, otherwise 1 mark for a correct method**)
5. $\frac{1}{10}$ of 30 = 3, so $\frac{6}{10}$ of 30 = 6 × 3 = 18. So Kyle wanted 18 tiles to be grey. 15 tiles in the picture are grey, so 18 − 15 = 3 more tiles should have been grey.
   (**2 marks for the correct answer, otherwise 1 mark for a correct method**)

Test 12 – pages 24-25

1. a) 65 should be circled. (**1 mark**)
   b) 59 should be circled. (**1 mark**)
2.
   ```
   a)   1 6 5        b)   9 3 7
      + 3 3 7           − 5 1 1
      ───────           ───────
        5 0 2             4 2 6
        ¹ ¹
   ```
   (**2 marks for all four correct digits, otherwise 1 mark for two or more correct digits**)
3. Between them Ruthie and Gina get $\frac{3}{8} + \frac{2}{8} = \frac{5}{8}$ of the pack of balloons. One whole pack is $\frac{8}{8}$, so Eli gets $\frac{8}{8} - \frac{5}{8} = \frac{3}{8}$ of the pack of balloons.
   (**2 marks for the correct answer, otherwise 1 mark for a correct method**)
4. Keiron buys 6 × 2 = 12 pens, so Sean also buys 12 pens. So Sean must buy 12 ÷ 3 = 4 packs. (**1 mark**)
5. Each mark is worth 100 ÷ 2 = 50 ml. So the jug contains 300 + 50 = 350 ml of squash. After Kim pours out 150 ml, there is 350 − 150 = 200 ml of squash left, and after Jack pours some squash there is 100 ml left. So Jack pours out 200 − 100 = 100 ml of squash.
   (**2 marks for the correct answer, otherwise 1 mark for a correct method**)

Progress Chart

That's all the tests in the book done — nice one!

Now fill in this table with all of your scores and see how you got on.

	Score
Test 1	
Test 2	
Test 3	
Test 4	
Test 5	
Test 6	
Test 7	
Test 8	
Test 9	
Test 10	
Test 11	
Test 12